Contents

KU-754-496

Getting ready

Grandma shows us how to make barfi.

At school

It's fun getting ready for Divali at school.

Our shrine

Don't you think our shrine looks beautiful?

Now it is time to do puja.

We are very careful when I light my diva.

Super sweets

We mustn't forget to buy some special sweets.

Looking our best

Mummy is very good at making mehndi patterns.

A family gathering

My cousin is ready for our **party**.

What a lovely feast!

Presents

Happy Divali!

Playing games

We all play a special Divali game and eat lots of sweets!

There are games and stick dancing at the mandir.

Divali lights

Don't the Divali lights in the mandir look pretty?

There are lots of **firework** displays.

Index

The end

Notes for adults

Most festivals and celebrations share common elements that will be familiar to the young child, such as new clothes, special food, sending and receiving cards and presents, giving to charity, being with family and friends and a busy and exciting build-up time. It is important that the child has an opportunity to compare and contrast their own experiences with those of the children in the book. This will be helped by asking the child open-ended questions, using phrases like: What do you remember about …? What did we do …? Where did we go …? Who did we see …? How did you feel …?

Divali takes place in October or November. It is a festival of light celebrated by Hindus (and some Sikhs, although the celebrations are slightly different). Streets and homes are decorated with candles and coloured lights and there are often spectacular firework displays. Special prayers (puja) are said, new clothes are worn, presents are exchanged and there are community gatherings at the temple (mandir).

Follow up activities could include making a Divali card for a Hindu friend, reading a children's version of the story of Rama and Sita, finding a recipe and making barfi (coconut sweetmeats) and decorating a room by lighting it only with tea-lights and candles.